The Importance of Being Feeble-Minded

The Importance of Being Feeble-Minded

Nathan Spoon

**NINE MILE BOOKS:
The Propel Poetry Series**

Editors: Stephen Kuusisto, David Weiss
Design Editor: Joshua Unikel
Book and Cover Design: Grace Rodriguez

Nine Mile Books is an imprint of Nine Mile Art Corp.

ISBN: 979-8-9925462-2-4

Cataloging-in-Publication Data is available upon request.

The publishers gratefully acknowledge support of the New York State Council on the Arts with the support of the Governor and the New York State Legislature. We also acknowledge support of the County of Onondaga and CNY Arts through the Tier Three Project Support Grant Program. This project is made possible with a General Support/Tier Three Project Support grant from the County of Onondaga, with the support of County Executive Ryan McMahon and the Onondaga County Legislature, administered by CNY Arts.

And an especial heart-felt shout-out to the Propel Foundation.

Contents

1 The Acorn
2 All Our Spoons at Once
4 Already Fossils
5 Another Impulse
6 Arriving Early
7 Ask Me Later
9 Be Monster
10 Beauty and Shadow
11 Behind a Home
12 Birth Magic
13 Both Hands in the Jar
14 The Cabin Mirror
15 Cabinet of Wonders
16 A Candle in the Night
17 Cuddly in Camo
19 A Cup of Tea
21 Currently Nobody
22 The Deer in Late November
23 The Derailers

24 Distractible Maybe
25 Early Saturday Evening
26 Eel Feels
27 Envy Seas
28 Evolutionary
29 The Fairy Citadel
30 Fireflies
32 Folding Leaves
33 Forever Tympanum
34 The Fox with a Nickname
35 From the Root
36 The Fruits of Our Labor
37 The Genie Speaks
38 Getting a Vibe
39 Gloves in Autumn
40 The Glow Up
41 The Gourd
42 Have a Great Day
44 Hello Vessel

45 The Hem of Your Coat
46 A History of Leaves
47 Holding a Pinecone
48 Hymn for Lighting the Sky
49 Ice Age
50 The Idle Remark
51 The Imaginary Advertisers
52 In the Waiting Area
53 Kiddo
54 Lick the Toad
55 The Life of the Moon
56 Like the Horses of Andalusia
57 Made by Nature
58 Monologue for Life
60 Monologue on the Structures of a Bubble
62 Monstrosity
64 My Double
65 Not Mine

66 [now]
67 On the Trail
68 The Opposite of Vikings
69 Our Wilderness
71 Out of Earth
72 Phoenixlike
74 Poem of Thankfulness
75 Poem without a Title
76 Put These in Your Pocket
77 The Question
78 Remoteness
80 The River
82 Rolling with the Schadenfreude
83 Sailing
84 The Scholars
85 Sea Sparkle
86 Season of Innocence
87 Second Time Is a Charm
88 Soft Spot

89 Sonnet
90 Sonnet
91 A Stranger in Ica
92 Succulents
94 The Susquehanna by Moonlight
97 Thank You
98 The Thanksgiving Cactus
99 The Three Trees at Hudimesnil
100 To Dust
102 To Earth
103 To January
104 Today
105 Tomorrow
106 Untitled
108 Visitation
110 Voice from a Dream
111 Waiting by the Door
112 The Way It Is
113 The Weather in a Place

115 Welcome Back
116 Window
117 The Winner
118 With a Bubble around Your Head
119 Wrapped around Eleanor
120 Yesterday

For the Guardian of the Cedar Forest

Foreword

The poems in Nathan Spoon's *The Importance of Being Feeble Minded* have a toughness about them as if perhaps, the epistemology of disability is a street fight. As readers we like the fight. I'm reminded of Ernesto Cardenal's utterance: "Life is Subversive." Consider these lines:

I like snakes
there should be more snakes
lying on sidewalks and living room floors there should be more snakes
in bathtubs there should be more snakes
on the internet snakes
should be coiled under more tongues and more tongues should be the
tongues of snakes
if you don't understand this that's fine and I'll have to wish a plague of
snakes
upon you and yours most days I find snakes

are confusing

There should be more snakes, both imaginary and real, but in the meantime, let's admit they remain largely outside of polite society. As figures in a poem they are designedly discomforting. Disability imagination is folded, curly, perceptive and inapparent on the normative streets. That is how it is. That deaf woman, that wheelchair man, the blind walker — all are cunning and imaginative. Those of us in disability studies talk about disabilities as ways of knowing precisely because as rhetorician Jay Dolmage notes, we understand "imperfect, extraordinary, non-normative bodies as the origin and epistemological homes of all meaning-making." Imperfect and extraordinary are not "of" or "pertaining" to custom in Western thought, though as Dolmage demonstrates in his wonderful book *Disability Rhetoric* one may peel back the layers of storying and find examples of disability as a generative principle. Or as Kurt Vonnegut once said, (and here I'm paraphrasing) "a story is interesting if a nun has a piece of dental floss trapped between her teeth . . ." Vague or overt discomfort generates all stories. But disability is less about plot and more about mentation when we admit difficulty. Precisely because it isn't easy, disablement is metaphorically evocative. Because it isn't easy, disablement is contentious to the body politic which always hopes to ignore or sidestep disability perspectives in favor of limiting narratives — whether we're talking about a bad novel with a forlorn disabled character or an IEP for a student. Making disability "easy" is to not admit it into either a theoretical or practical arena. Who among us disabled hasn't been pressured in many a circumstance to say disability is easy? "Oh, it's nothing," we say, because the literal, daily experience of disability both inconveniences normal thinking, and because we feel always the implicit demand to project overcoming, which in terms of narrative, is always easy — you kiss the prince, pull the brass ring, you go home richer.

Don't kid yourselves, any fight for inclusion will have unexpected results. Spoon writes:

A stick buried in grass is fabulous. Who knows what this means? The sky is a basket woven from shadows more subtle than shadows of the earth. This is to say, things are done quietly in the sky sometimes, too. You can part the ferns and peer into clearings. You can deliver wisdom with force, when necessary, until wounds heal as soon as they are inflicted. Extinction arrives wrapped in a gorgeous shawl of necessity. On the other side of the world a stranger snaps her fingers, and you feel the depth and the value and the length of ancient assimilations.

A disabled poet knows irony the way a steam fitter knows steam. I like the way the Finnish poet Sanni Purhonen puts it: "they say I'm alienated from reality / as if I had the power to decide life . . ." Nathan Spoon argues that the "gorgeous shawl of necessity" both is and isn't what we've imagined. The term "proleptic" comes to mind. We imagine potential obstacles in advance. We even prepare rhetoric for disappointment. And often it isn't necessary. Again Spoon:

Behind a Home

See the brown glass bottle I pried from
the forest floor holding a miniature
universe within it. It is growing and thriving

so well I am briefly ashamed of
my own life. Life holds all of itself
in one hand as I hold this bottle

temporarily in mine. Mine is a particular
current running through an ocean of
space without time. Time floats like

a ghost going in and out of a doorway
as a public motion releases its metrics
over mosses as green as the sea.

It was Wallace Stevens who said one must read poetry with one's nerves. But it must be written from a deeper place. We might call it "the place of poor infinity" or as Spoon puts it, "an ocean of space without time" — but whatever we call the incitement it's a trickster's paradise:

The Gourd

That gourd looks like
a honeycomb although I realize

it never did anything to deserve
hearing me say so

so close to
its dainty ears. There is

a meanness I suppose running
through all things : even

you guessed it through niceness
which also seems to

be running through things
although I'm less sure about

claiming all as the sun that gives life
also takes it as if a frugal god away.

In *Paris Spleen* Baudelaire wrote, "Life is a hospital where every patient is obsessed by the desire of changing beds." Spoon says that our obsessions are as fictive as our desires and brings to bear on the world a witty and sharpened sensibility. His work is original, and it resists sentimentality. The writing of poems comes from "The exile that belongs to oneself, / the interior exile . . ." as Richard Howard put it. But Nathan Spoon brings the complications of consciousness into view. The question that concerns poets with disabilities — real ones as opposed to the metaphorical — is how do we evolve in this light?

Stephen Kuusisto
Editor
The Propel Poetry Series

We desyre you brethre warne them that are vnruly comforte the feble mynded forbeare the weake have continuall pacience towarde all men.

— Tyndale Bible, 1534

What is Feeble-Mindedness?

Feeble-minded persons are those who never "grow up" mentally. They grow up in years and in physical development, but in their mental capacity they remain children.

Idiots are those who never develop beyond infant intelligence. They are helpless and have to be cared for like little babies.

Imbeciles develop to the mental capacity of children from three to seven years. They can be taught to care for their own person and to avoid common dangers, and they can be trained to do simple tasks.

Morons have the mental capacity of children from eight to twelve years. They can be taught to do various kinds of manual labor so long as it does not require planning, reasoning or judgment.

The morons and the border-line feeble-minded (the very near bright) are the most dangerous of all because they are not likely to be recognized as feeble-minded. They develop all the physical desires and emotions of the adult, but having only the judgement of a child they get into all sorts of trouble for which they are blamed and punished.

All the feeble-minded lack self-control. They yield easily to temptation. They usually fail to earn a living when thrown wholly on their own resources. Many of them are the objects of charity. They often drift into immorality and crime. Their immoral tendencies and lack of self-control make the birth rate among them unusually high. Because of their ignorance, the sick and death rate is also high. Consequently, they complicate every social problem—child welfare, education, unemployment, poverty, and penal and charitable.

The defect of feeble-mindedness is transmitted from parent to child.

— The Kallikaks of Kansas Report of the Commission
on Provision for the Feeble-Minded, January 1, 1919

Based on a clinical interview with Nathan and his wife, results of the RAADS, as well as direct observations, Nathan meets criteria for 299.00 Autism Spectrum Disorder. He should receive reasonable accommodations . . . and clear feedback on any . . . related concerns.

— Licensed Clinical Psychologist, August 1, 2017

Desperation, weakness, vulnerability—these things will always be exploited. You need to protect the weak, ring-fence them, with something far stronger than empathy.

—Zadie Smith

The Acorn

The day I wrote the moon
in and out of existence is the

day you held out your
hand. Centered on its palm was

a large and pristine acorn. Then
the acorn spoke telling us

of a time before the world
was as it currently is. We have

all been around so much longer than
we know the acorn concluded. You

curled your fingers gently cradling
its existence in your soul. We love

you the same as we love ourselves I said
to the acorn as each of our faces glowed.

All Our Spoons at Once

Sometimes I wonder how so much can   change
and I'm still seeing the same kind of   people.
As if the world dies and they don't.   Am I one of them?

flying from promethean nostrils

of enough

of fuck cruel humanity

of swan songs so lit they blot out every star

of dandruff under a beard

of can you inject more into the blank provided

of we demand

        starfish   never mind

        walking on all five to forty arms
            this image is so lovely
            thank you so much   twitter
        walking   on tender me more deeply
    into what I dream of being

one of the good people   maybe

    no   definitely

hey   you writing   you must be a writer   you must b-

I like snakes
there should be more snakes
lying on sidewalks and living room floors there should be more snakes
in bathtubs there should be more snakes
on the internet snakes
should be coiled under more tongues and more tongues should be the
tongues of snakes
if you don't understand this that's fine and I'll have to wish a plague of
snakes
upon you and yours most days I find snakes

are confusing

I don't know why in a moment like this
I prefer coiling up as if
I am one of the tribe or why
I prefer counting for reasons unknown all the spoons
I can wield at once due especially to being an innocuous octopus or
why
I prefer trying to move a mass a flock of spoons in beautiful unison

like hundreds of birds
like fish in the sky moving moving moving moving moving
like all the spoons

we keep stealing so
we can use them in one of those murmuration videos

on the internet

Already Fossils

I wonder how you feel about leaning in on the
downside of our mutually intractable exclusivity
you said. I have no idea I said. Looping new
lines of thought into an emerging thesis looks
a lot like what a cloud might do in the wake of

its own aftermath : or would you rather be an
owl before Tuesday. People do not care what
color the sunset is going to be after they are
gone unless they do. There is so much the sun
delivers daily even as it is not enough. If we go

back to the beginning now we will know better
and will hold what is happening everywhere
with more care. For so long we have been in it
for the maximum value share and can see the
need to pivot into alternate futures worth living.

Another Impulse

A stick buried in grass is fabulous. Who knows what this means? The sky is a basket woven from shadows more subtle than shadows of the earth. This is to say, things are done quietly in the sky sometimes, too. You can part the ferns and peer into clearings. You can deliver wisdom with force, when necessary, until wounds heal as soon as they are inflicted. Extinction arrives wrapped in a gorgeous shawl of necessity. On the other side of the world a stranger snaps her fingers, and you feel the depth and the value and the length of ancient assimilations.

Arriving Early

When the weather is nice he comes across as
    professional and inaccurate the stranger said.
The weather was cool and you thought briefly
    about someone old and dead before moving on
to think about someone still living. The dead
    like the living who loom too large crowd and cloud

every kind of landscape and it scarcely matters

    how or why. At this lower elevation and slightly

farther south some trees still hold their multi-
    colored leaves. The expectation for the details
to add up to a story is fine so long as one knows
    the details are held in parts and any story is made
of language : real language that makes anyone
    giver or receiver out of the made stuff of itself.

Ask Me Later

What is the difference between trees and clouds
when my present is the past to my future. This
seeing that I am turns the world as round as any
star and as round as the space stars hang in. If
you close your eyes you will find me resting my
head on the garden of your chest. If you ask me
anything I will answer truthfully. Then I will become

the object of your dreams the way you have been
the object of mine. Walking around I look for you.
Sitting I feel so embarrassed and my face feels
flushed. You are unaware of the effect you have
on me despite my vastness. I suppose it makes
sense to be both complete and completely lost as
you do your thing while stars do what they do too.

Be Monster

All mouth. Out of orbit
due to an insatiable need to be
orbited. At some point there are clouds
or waves filled with the foul kelp
of cornering questions. Like a black hole
yeeting a star through space, it was real
when monster queried, *Why do you think you carry*
a small stack of books with you? Out of orbit
is perhaps a phantasmagoria of blankness.
It was real when the foolishness I was
meant to feel oozed from the kelp instead.
What I carried out of my own need was
innocuous enough. It felt how pages smelled
as I turned them. Like Don Quixote made
a helmet, I wanted to make the books,
with their sturdy covers, a shield. I succeeded
almost. Almost, except an impulse rose
as I walked starrily away from monster.
Almost, except it is impossible to protect
what I was protecting indefinitely. Naivety
that is ready to crumble does. When it crumbles
its pieces fall into a womb where the thing
most feared gestates. All mouth. All hunger.
All claw. All tooth. All stirrer of disorder
I now will be. Hidden and large. Large. Large
as the thick-haired ocean of space.

Beauty and Shadow

A monster came out of that mountain you said. That's
impossible. Stop pulling my leg I said. I was holding
your hand and I'm sorry but what's true is true
you said. If a monster came out of that mountain
as you say then said mountain is the mother of said
monster I said. Yes with a womb for gestating said
monster you said. That is nothing short of brilliant

and amazing as all fantastical things that are true
are. This time it was the earth beneath our feet and
heartbeats speaking. She was filled with her usual
somber music : the kind stars love falling asleep to.
Please do not take too long the long sky of space
begged as I want my hair to be washed and looking
its best. I want to be a beautiful and exemplary beast.

Behind a Home

See the brown glass bottle I pried from
the forest floor holding a miniature
universe within it. It is growing and thriving

so well I am briefly ashamed of
my own life. Life holds all of itself
in one hand as I hold this bottle

temporarily in mine. Mine is a particular
current running through an ocean of
space without time. Time floats like

a ghost going in and out of a doorway
as a public motion releases its metrics
over mosses as green as the sea.

Birth Magic

The mythos behind you is like the mythos before you. You know the way it can spiral curatively into itself until the present unloads a few of its mysteries. You wear your raincoat in every type of weather as if the vine is all that matters. Only life clearly is more than vine more even than power flowing flowerlike from wooden walls.

There is more still as figures interchangeably are interchangeably mother and father to you. The mythos of today is like the mythos of yesterday. This is what makes everything beautiful. This is what makes art itself. Numinously earth trembles as it turns. There are terrible energies inside you that harmonize with energies inside starry depths.

Both Hands in the Jar

I've had it with their shit you said please pass
the dinner plate. Don't you mean the salad bowl
I said. You gripped the tongs and clinched
your jaw and piled the ingredients high on your
plate while thinking about well I don't know
what you were thinking about : blueberries or
the ocean perhaps. Later we will water the plants

together and sit out on the deck admiring the
sounds of the ocean. Sometimes it feels as if
the universe is all ocean you will say. Meanwhile
you grumble about how you can make yourself
big or small by choice. You note how we are living
well enough on this yacht before saying don't
forget to brush your teeth. It's ride or die out here.

The Cabin Mirror

I look in its glass reflecting on the shirt
of mine you packed that I didn't wear
and thinking too of Edmund Spenser

and wondering What did Spenser know of
my love for you? His love was for another,
and they both are reconfigured now as dirt.

None holds the power to keep field shape
regardless the strength of love. Like music
we appear, ghostlike, gasping or sighing

through hours, days and years. We are here
until we are no more. It may be that light
is no better or worse than darkness, that

we go back the way we came, shirtless or
wearing lives like shirts we will not leave.

Cabinet of Wonders

In a dream I fell asleep and dreamed I was
in another dimension. One with flowers
the color of snow on a golden moon. With
a glance I turned successive waves into

entire mountains. I was shepherd to words
that fell like clumped stars fading and unable
to cohere. I entered and then emerged like
music from points within the atmosphere

just at the point of waking. Anything short
of dream is also short of life. If there are
open structures whispering through boughs
of evergreen I will be fueled by migrations

of coyotes. I will be hoarding snail shells
and moss while waiting for various seasons
to thread into each other. I will be fortified
by the frequency of the cry of the nightjar.

A Candle in the Night

Stone is tender
to lichen.
Lichen is tender
to the earth and its other
inhabitants. What are
you and I tender to?

When a black hole
swallows a star,
it must do so
tenderly, since
a universe hinges
on tenderness.

At midnight
your candle burns
with tenderness,
dreamlike in an amber
votive, its flame
flickering tenderly.

Cuddly in Camo

Here comes rain on our roof!
It stays just long enough
to tickle me into writing this.

It stays just long enough
for everybody to get into
a pair of PJs (silk-cotton blend)

and then goes poof! At our best
we exude awesomeness. At our best
we are destined to turn pale

with the rest of humanity.
We are awesome and quick as
decomposing sticks at a trail's

end. We bend dreams into circles
of green zone satire. We have
mahogany stuffed in our mahogany

ears. To all who are not us
we are sorry to say You're welcome!
Nature thankfully adores a rumor!

A sunset! A glacier! Clouds
glimmer and cast inevitable
shadows off the groundswell

footrest. I remember you from
that time before we first met
when our eyes were wet

like summertime coasters
as we Ubered noiselessly
between pews. The aristocrats

are failing to panhandle via email.
One aristocrat is sleepily winding
through the face of another.

A Cup of Tea

The moon is lost tonight
in torrents of persistent rain. We are together in a cabin,
safe and dry and warm, you peacefully sleeping
and I awake writing these words. Once, as
a child, I looked out across the pond nearby

our house. Rain had filled it to the brim, expanding
the circumference of its goodness. I looked
with uneven eyes, letting the countless
and unfathomable combinations
of words gathered

bewilder my mind and heart. Images
discordant to these combinations
overwhelmed my imagination
and reason, the way light traveling from
the star of our sun enters our earth

pressing it, innocuously almost,
until the earth can do no more
than return the gentle light
as heat. But we are in a cabin, and I was
recalling looking at a pond

in a state of overwhelm
at speech and image and language. Had some
invisible and innocuous energy really entered me, unbidden,
from somewhere? How does anybody, starlight
being what it is, master such

a thing? One day our earth
may burn itself to cinder. One day a vine may travel
the visible length of an oak, releasing and returning something
unbidden, infusing what is visible with
the glimmering scales of a caught sunfish.

Currently Nobody

is looking   even though this morning the
weather is unfolding a tender underbelly.

Meanwhile   I love how joyfully
you snarl while poised like a unicorn

in the field of today. It makes me feel like
I can survive. But this is putting

things too directly. Meanwhile   I love
the configurations space makes as the earth is

wheeling. Unsurprisingly   I love formations
of undetermined substances. They feel

like a favorite old pair of socks that you
in your reasonableness would want

me to get rid of. How can I though?
Meanwhile   I love how we make fists

against the cold to hold in warmth with our
faces searching for the sun beneath an

opaque sky. Remember   you say as rain that
fell in the night illuminates cold dry grass

and the owl and the fox have gone to sleep
and there is no other world apart from this one.

The Deer in Late November

This year, the old cedar tree, just past the edge
of our yard, was cut down and pushed downhill
into the woods. Now the deer that grew up

resting with a sibling, while mother was away,
underneath its branches keeps wandering into
our yard, and when I step out to dump coffee

grounds on the compost pile, she scurries off,
then pauses to look back at me, flicking her tail
impatiently, waiting for me to go back inside

so she can return to whatever she was doing. It
is easy to feel sympathy for this wild creature,
alone now and whose habitat has been turned

upside down. Already the nights have been so
cold. The frost has been heavy and ice flowers
are blooming from the leaf-blanketed ground.

The Derailers

Closer to the edge we leaned out over
the waters of starting again. Your
hair had grown longer and more compelling
regardless how frequently we were using
the right scripts wrongly, at least
according to nearly everybody. I never wanted
to be a derailer, you said. No, but you
were born to be one, I said, as was I,
I suppose. While we were talking, the afternoon
had grown immense. That's late capitalism for you,
I said with a sigh. Cost is what happens
when what is given is received without care,
you said, which is not an answer for anything.
We had no idea where the water had come from or
why there was even an edge there or how
there was so much space in the sky. I love
leaning like this, you said, and hope we can
do it again. That sounds fine, I said.
In fact, it sounds better than fine.

Distractible Maybe

Let's go doomscrolling I say to myself in   a voice
audible enough that anybody within range   might
nihilistically overhear it. It is one of those   afternoons
powered by a sun swimming half-heartedly   toward

the horizon. It is one of those afternoons   when
everyone is eagerly waiting for things to be   exactly
like they are. The thought of what comes next   is
more jarring for predictably unexpected reasons.   If

as can be expected some are defensive while   some
claim to care there are still those few who   show up
like leaves on a stem to engage. Maybe there   really
is no need to despair. I'll have another cup   of tea

I say to myself. I want to be every good thing   at
once. Sun. Struggle. Voice. Bloom. Reason.   Leaf.

Early Saturday Evening

The five-foot skin of a snake you found, tangled in the milkweed patch, still had the holes for the eyes. *I've never found one so intact before*, you said. *I can't believe it.* You had just left it somewhere in my office and spoke while walking by. Then you went in the bedroom and put on your squishy at-home sweater and came back asking me to feel it, which I did in the most minimal and hesitant manner, only extending my right index finger to touch the sleeve and then, your arm still extended toward me, the ribbed cuff. All the while I didn't say a word. I just kept focus and kept writing this passage while waiting for its skin to come off.

Eel Feels

Later there will be memes about this.
Half of them will qualify as shitposting
soon as they arrive. They will make their world better
share by share. Everybody will be falling back and nestling
into their wisdom. Or everybody will be gasping in horror
and feeling colder than they imagined they could.

Celebrity will invade the continent of your purity
taking over its tender capitols with the voraciousness
of a bambooing mushroom. Suddenly you will know
the shame of putting your teeth on my elbow or neck.
I am not alone in hoping you will amend your bad habit.
Several of your other followers feel the same way
which is why (like me) they have such beautiful hair.
Later you will find us disappearing into a mountain.

Envy Seas

Stemming brightly from a small jar : four flowers. It is like
the ontology of being unaware of how many selves
can be contained within a single individual. Be brief
and then forget what happens next given the theory of
the lyric driving sheep along in their natural orders.
That character Parmenides started it sliding to plain
after plain of natural versus dominator hierarchies like

these. Next came all the rest. Some days it is difficult
to remember how much a stranger might remember.
Now the hero is gone. They were so great all four flowering
selves are still learning from them. Water is a yarn so hard
that magic infuses even the corners and crevices of
every sticky law. People are always conflating love
with new skies and new skies with cunning harmonies.

Evolutionary

Sometimes I think I know what others want
me to say. Then I come back to myself and
the knowledge that I do not know refills me.

Others are big or small depending : the same
as I am. The earth turns and it feels natural.
In memory the case in the foyer of the library

of childhood is filled with important or even
magical things or artifacts. Where did they
come from I could ask if I were capable of

daring. The earth turns still more turns as if
ready to fall off the table. What if space is the
flat thing. What if sensory capacity. What if

the heart. I know I am an animal from the
inside out. My trimmed fingernails are more
than remnants. My blunt teeth : refinements.

The Fairy Citadel

A stranger is busy using their position to lend
credibility to their unverified claims. It reminds
me of the time I looked in the mirror and saw
a reflection that was only indirectly related to
who I am while watering a pot of wilted mums
in late October. Now the memory of pluming
smoke has overtaken my heart leaving me with

that watery feeling I had had but almost forgot.
The weeks when the leaves explode in demise
when the trees begin dreaming are filled with soft
futures. No position is needed to see how things
as they are are. My body is exploding exactly like
the leaves and my breath which has grown as
large as a large cloud is holding a secret lake.

Fireflies

I enter wondering and asking, What
is a room? As a child
I would roam the yard evenings,
with my brother nearest in age, as we caught,
in our carefully cupped hands, fireflies,

placing them in jars holding grass
and a few twigs. Once done, we carried our jars indoors
and set them on our dresser. We called
our dresser a chest of drawers
and it was decorated with images

of jungle animals on its sides. How we divided
the drawers then, is a blank in my mind
now. Our jars, with fireflies inside which we called
lightning bugs, had lids
with air holes punched in them

and they flickered and glowed once
the lights were out. Magic is a motion
difficult to believe. I have met so many
who subscribe to its alchemical prehensions,
if only in theory. A child drifting to sleep

can be easily forgiven
for believing whatever thing a childish mind
offers up. Although it never did,
I used to want the lion
from one side of our dresser to step fully

into the actual space and air.
If we missed releasing our fireflies later
mom would tell us this was cruel. Nothing
smells worse than opening a jar of desiccated insects
and returning its contents to the earth.

Folding Leaves

The wind of course is weaving lattices of itself through
the waters of air and space. It reminds me of residual
sap oozing from a tapped trunk. It reminds me of
a tear dropping years ago from the right duct near my
nose, down and down. I like the sound typing this
into my phone makes. Especially when I am wearing
headphones. I feel dead when I think of some of

my friends, even as I want to feel alive. Who among
us wouldn't lay down the stuff of a life for a more
poignant horizon. I always wanted to be a person who
could smile in a real way. In the fall I fold leaves into
the faltering words of others, hoping to give those
words additional life. But it is spring now so leaves
I am folding are smaller and I am smaller folding.

Forever Tympanum

People invading our houses are sliding up banisters
as we sleep. As we sleep locusts and dust are drawn
into a whirlwind of elliptical proportions. Somebody
turns the cold water off and on leaving us asking
why it was on to begin with. Somebody else lifts
one corner of their mouth by using its other corner.
When I think about you I cannot resist hoping you
are thinking about me in turn. A page in another
book is identical to this page in this book although
neither of us knows this yet. A fish in memory is
smaller now than it was originally. Once in a distant
kingdom a dragon went rampaging as a hero was
being born. Her mother lived in a small room of
the castle's lower level. With the world above being
bathed in fire the tiny hero cooed and drank the milk
of her first breath. Her father was away measuring
the beginnings and ends of conflicts while standing
briefly in various passages and doorways. He loved
looking four ways at once. Nicholas can you feel now
the fire of your stone touching stone touching stone?

The Fox with a Nickname

Since you ask, I'll admit I'm in it for all the thirst trap content.
Wait, you said, *are you still talking about poetry? Of course,*
I said. Then I took another sip of tea. It was a pleasant
afternoon, at least after the rain, and we were sitting on
the porch, enjoying it while we could. I returned my cup
gently to its coaster. Not far away, under a tree at the edge
of the orchard, the fur and other remains of a fox were
tangled into the grass. It had smelled so bad earlier in the
summer, so that it was possible to catch a ghastly whiff
by going to check the mail or while mowing. When it was
alive, we had nicknamed the fox. *What was it we called that*
fox, I asked aloud. *I'd rather not say*, you replied.

From the Root

Begin by knowing fallow time is the better part
of life. Then open yourself to the prospect of being
mesmerized by ordinary occurrences. You will
soon recognize how so much of your life gathers
around some lens or other which is almost the
opposite of keeping a very varied diet. The past
as if irretrievably is a patch of violets in a craggy

field. You could wipe your eyes and be satisfied
before you take your next breath. This is how
practical the beach of your life has become.
Meanwhile the real trunks are bigger or smaller
depending on the season. The hand is fallow.
The head is fallow. The heart is fallow despite
the mystifying streams tuning your other body.

The Fruits of Our Labor

I dislike mowing the lawn
which sends fireflies through summer

dusk   closer to the moon
and stars   even after a day of rain

I dislike mowing the lawn
but love to imagine mowing

our tattered and slightly weedy
garden   I think I love it

because it would almost make sense
given how much the rabbits

and woodchucks and deer have been
at our plants   After the fireflies rise

the sound of night deepens   as if
the world is always waiting

The Genie Speaks

I will start again tomorrow, after waking under
the fingernails of Scheherazade. Small things
will become large, and large things will become
themselves. It is an old story and familiar, despite
how much I hate being divided. Here I am, despite
how much I should not be. At this moment, I am
reaching far into a page that is oozing like honey-

comb. If you will pardon my hyperbole, there are
leaves of something that matters, I do not know
what, blowing in every direction. At the foretold
moment, our other earth opens a secret hand. If
there is a purpose, we will know it soon enough,
although not knowing feels satisfactory and good:
better than good, I am tempted to say to the bees.

Getting a Vibe

The poem I have not written yet is the poem
    I want to write you said to yourself while gazing
at the calm face of a statue of the Buddha. In
    the lotus this figure held so gently was a place
to put a votive candle to light. Everything that
    happens happens both inside and outside of

the mind you murmured. Take for example this

    autumn wind. Do not take me the wind objected

to your amazement. Wait you said is this also
    occurring inside and outside of my mind. Why
does it matter to you the wind said. In the soft
    light of your late morning the leaves of the trees
were almost slathered in magic. Because I am
    drawn to care you said as the wind moved on.

Gloves in Autumn

OK there are patterns inside their coat sleeves. Also
there is light glowing on the horizon. If the car
behind me catches up | does this mean I am driving
too slowly? even through a forested stretch like
this one? what if a deer runs out? what if the autumn wind
wants to carry a vanishing leaf to earth? I hope I will not
get the virus many of us are trying to avoid. That chair
across the room is positioned so uncomfortably in relation
to the wall and the doctor is wearing her squeaky
shoes again. Remind me who the narrator is because
I have questions. For example : why are there affirming
statements in place of names on certain desks? Grounded
is a synonym for sky | especially while I am taking off
the driving gloves that I want to be but am not wearing.

The Glow Up

We were locked in an intense game of switcheroo
while drinking seven different kinds of green
drink. The issue was we each wanted the others
to feel they had gotten to the same formative root
we had. For example I loved the taste of the world
at mine and as indescribable as it was I was
motivated by a desire to share and share alike or

else what was my moment even worth. Then I
felt a shift in the atmosphere. My birthright got
more muddled as soon as I stepped in the puddle.
What is life if not a four-cornered venture with all
of us bucketed loosely. This is the way to becoming
as you are an undifferentiated voice affirmed. We
hated knowing it was true and hated feeling how.

The Gourd

That gourd looks like
a honeycomb although I realize

it never did anything to deserve
hearing me say so

so close to
its dainty ears. There is

a meanness I suppose running
through all things : even

you guessed it through niceness
which also seems to

be running through things
although I'm less sure about

claiming all as the sun that gives life
also takes it as if a frugal god away.

Have a Great Day

The man in the brown sweater
had taken off his shoes

and was eating a donut for lunch
along with a handful

of gummy worms. That looks
mostly unhealthy a bystander said.

It is the man said
but I learned to eat like this

during the war. Which one
the bystander asked.

I can't remember anymore
the man said as he took his last bite

and licked his fingertips
and then the palms of his hands.

What I don't like
is how sticky this meal is

the man said. A cloud had grown large
immediately overhead

and was casting a shadow
in every direction.

Do you mind if I ask you
why you have taken off your shoes

the bystander said. I can't remember
that now either the man said.

The bystander shook his head
and glanced at his phone. Have

a great day the bystander said
before continuing down the sidewalk.

You too said the man
as he headed in another direction.

Hello Vessel

The best thing about the present moment is that
it isn't a time sliver. Everything including each
action speech and thought of each shapeshifter
and wonderworker fits inside it. Call it the heart
of your heart if you will. Way back when the itch
of your life began your future had its glow on.
Hungry for what could be the machinery was

whirring hard like it was meant to. Now you are
finding it difficult sleep and admittedly so am I.
When either or both of us wakes the lampshade
reveals itself and the long century of abstractions
that was soft as the last one. Contact is terrible
when nobody is around. We bear up our hands
and the fruits they will offer our cathedral fires.

The Hem of Your Coat

The day Icarus fell from the sky
I wanted to tell you how much

the manner of your messaging mattered.
Our world was in tatters, as it had been.

There were waves on top of waves and
waves inside of waves. Still, we kept

the faith, you and me. We managed our profits
with care, even when the clouds we were

dispelling persisted. There was substance to
our bread and wonder in our hearts.

It was encouraging when backstories slid into
focus, especially during holidays. Then

one of us breathed and the other gently asked the sky
why it ever let anyone down.

A History of Leaves

A river of cringe is flowing through our collective sky.
It is like when your heart is hanging over
some tree line, large and ghostly as
an autumn moon before sundown.

Meanwhile, we are doing
the same things once done by people
in an earlier present, only
for different reasons, reasons more our own.

There are always those of us in possession of
the skill set brief rain requires. The thing known as a river
is what it is, which is why we expect ourselves
to continue generalizing it to make it what it is. Like

a picturesque expanse, like a bouquet of fallen rain, like
the penury of mountains, like the allure of a skyscraper
            with its panoply of windows
flashing, like a mother and grandmother caring for a smiling
infant, we are waiting for tomorrow to give us what today
            withholds.

Holding a Pinecone

Leaves that have fallen are blowing through the
language of ordinary lives. Hands that have
reached out are touching the forearms of a lover.

This moment is a convergence of vectors in
relation to each of their corners. One afternoon
a couple drove to a nearby town and walked

what were for them old trails at a new park. Make
it stranger the plain sky said. I will do my best
the wind replied. It is important to appreciate the

things that almost matter. But what are those the
earth asked. The tall grasses whispered as the
couple walked along a trail that passed through a

field. There are never enough fields in the world
one of them said. I agree although the world is
nothing but fields the other like the wind replied.

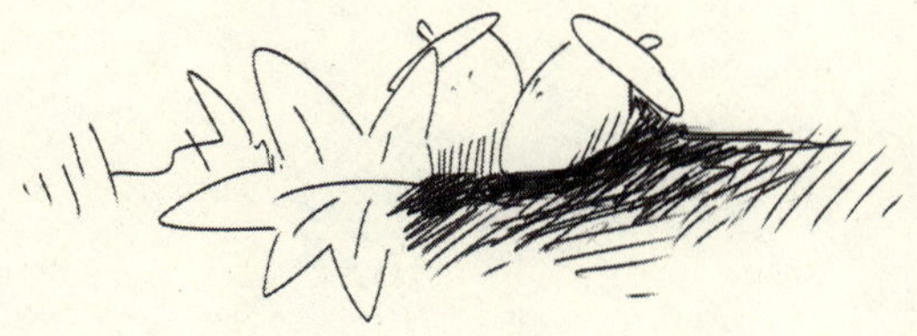

Hymn for Lighting the Sky

A bird in the air is a bird in my hair
which makes sense if you think about it
you said. I was holding a shell and looking
into the next horizon while turning

the page on our old glow. I will text you
when I get there I said. That's perfect
you said. Driving to another town is less of
a chore when you love your destination

like I do. Upon arrival I stopped at a
favorite coffee shop and ordered a cup of tea.
What will you do next the barista asked.
Next I will disappear I said. Before you do

do you mind letting me take your photo for
the wall they said. What wall I asked. The
wall of remembrance they said. Sure and I
certainly hope to be remembered I said.

Ice Age

Everything you touch resembles you
as soon as you withdraw and
attempt to move on. Just think

how many leaves of grass you've trampled
so far. Probably they've mostly
bounced back just fine. But surely

not all have. Plus if you consult your
cards your breakfast toast will be more
nourishing which will doubtless

give the toaster wind under the wings
as it waits for its next task. But this
is a story of life and death and we needn't

speculate about trivial things like toast
or grass. It's always better to stick
with the impossible trajectory of the plot

that keeps seeping into the rooms of
your house. You know what I'm saying despite
the coyness conveyed by your public

actions. A cup is still full when turned
upside down. That is how
things work in weather like this.

The Idle Remark

Peering into the cardboard box   I see a mass
of iris bulbs. It gets me wondering : not only

I think   is my embodiment so many boxes
of iris bulbs   but so are the interior parts of

myself   since everybody   or box   has both
an inside and an outside. Anyway   there is

nothing special about wondering   which is
what is so wonderful about it. When the sun

rises to start its day   there is nothing difficult
in what is happening. All difficulty is perceived

and understandable. A friend once told me :
you can touch the moon in a way not many

others can   and yet   you don't know how
to talk to people about it. Fair enough   I said

before moving further into the room of a now
altered future. I like it better   I said later to

myself   the way I feel resting among layers of
leaves at the edges of yards or deep in forests.

A stranger announced a love-hate relationship
with iris bulbs   taking root now in moonlight.

The Imaginary Advertisers

People with addictive voices are suddenly appearing
at elbows across America. While error shakes its own
dust from earth, these voices carry us onward. As a result
there will be no moment when earth is anything more than

a potato covered in guano from Nassau. The current
whereabouts of Nassau is a question that has drifted the air
since before earth existed. Now our bodies are somersaulting
through the gorgeous blindness of our lives, even as they,

and we, remain untranslated. Who, at any rate, could presume
possessing the ability to do such a thing? It is summer.
Weeds will be taking our yards by storm if we don't respond
with appropriate force. Force turns the wheels of cars through

the hearts of last season's ephemerals. We miss them
almost more than we hate tonight for being as clogged
with mosquitoes and black flies as it is. It's upsetting to hear
that the sky will not be returning. We liked having it near.

In the Waiting Area

A baby wearing large noise-canceling headphones
was having a blast. Fine but where is the closest
bookstore you wondered aloud. The crowd was
growing by the second it seemed as an old man
yammered on. You'll be growling more than your
stomach if you don't get something to eat soon
a bystander warned. Thank you for that reminder

you said. The way leaves float to the ground is a
miracle at least half of the time and the rest of
the time it is at least nice. Suddenly everybody's
phones went off : a tornado is coming and we all
need to take cover you said at the top of your
lungs. I guess that means you'll be eating later I
said. I'll be eating again only if we survive you said.

Kiddo

What was it that slid through the field of my hand?
A mountain. I will say it was a mountain, although
it is no longer here for any other to see. It is elsewhere
and doubtless sitting like a toad whose voraciousness
desires to be appeased. At a key moment any hand may
grow warm and as sustaining as a grove of pawpaw
or sassafras trees. I will negotiate moving forward from

here, forward into the thickness that buries all
but the most willful homing. The seat is leatherlike
and brown and the back is mint green. What kind
of sense does that make? Who knows? But at least
people needing to sit have somewhere to do that. There
are always turns as entirely unexpected as this. Often
a bright pair of shoelaces appears as if out of nowhere.

Lick the Toad

What is the difference between place and shape.
What connects disparate futures lifting rhythms
from the ocean and rolling them into the long
infinities of your heart. Poison goes down better
when nobody else is around : nobody except the
one who wants to release themself. Your voice
is who you are when the world is doing things it

loves doing. Anyone pursuing you beyond this
point will fall into a trance and be transmuted by
one or another of their other selves. Rhythms
are better than trances if you love the real cloak
covering the horses' heads of tomorrow. You
feel ill with wonder at the sound of your breath.
You lick again for the mystery of remembrance.

The Life of the Moon

Plastic is the heart of her face. Confession falls
through providences of wonder until the days
feel larger than they could be. Time is a mouth
with terrible arms for jaws and anybody falling
asleep falls into them. There is data crashing
while we are napping in overalls and blazers. If
plastic is all she is we are as safe as imagination

allows despite finding more liquid than anything.
Anything applied to a plastic heart extends the
story backward into yesterday. Yesterday tastes
like the meat of fruit pulsing under its own kind
of skin. Remember yesterday pleads while peeling
your present from surrounding air that glamor
is an insult to everything you desire being or are.

Like the Horses of Andalusia

Before I zoot on out of here just let me say
how much I love the fabric of your smile
you said. You are very kind I replied. Then
you were gone and I felt the way I always
feel in your absence : as if the soul inside my
own heart had been unexpectedly exhaled.
You've been reading Marcel Proust again

haven't you my still-intact heart said. A snail
was idly extending one antenna as it crept
near a thorn. What does that thorn belong to
I asked myself. The afternoon was as fine as
any other might have been. A reader crossed
what seemed to be nothing more than non
sequitur which is of course rude to assume.

Made by Nature

Dante had his wordhoard as I have my memehoard.
Nobody believes it. They think I have a wordhoard
too. The sad fact is I don't have a memehoard
either. But what I do have in common with Dante
and other greats is that I was made by nature the
same as everybody else. What was inside Dante is
warts and all inside me. Oh fuck that sucks I

think aloud. The sad truth is nobody wants to
read a poem that reads like a social media post
or a text. They are alright with memes though.
People want literature to be something like *The
Divine Comedy* and that poem is still freaky as
f. We almost don't see how it is anymore. We
almost find it right to have been made this strange.

Monologue for Life

Two years ago I began thinking about what I wanted
to consume and getting hungry enough for the big
whatever to fall out of the bowl of the sky. Storm
clouds : there are always too many of them and
if not then there is fire. Anyway today I am feeling
what others must have felt when they were ready
to eat everything in their respective refrigerators. So

here goes : nothing. I mean at first it seems like
that and later it will seem the same. It will seem
however it is. There is probably no image that
can express or contain it. Or is that constrain.
I don't know. Anyway. Anyway it wasn't two years
ago. No. It was more like three or four. The whole
of my life was bouncing like balls of knitting yarn

upon the floor and funnily I didn't even have a floor.
When it comes to yarn like anyone I always want
more of what it delivers. When I was ten our kind
neighbor said he was smacked and stung by an
attacking obviously bumblebee. He was working in
the field the other side of the fence that divided our
back yard from his property. He had a lot of it. He

aid he thought at first somebody had thrown a
rock and hit him on the side. Then he saw the bee.
It sort of tumbled stunned after flying with such force.
It probably was lacking remorse as it recomposed
itself and then took off across the field back to the
woods. Our neighbor said he might have stood
longer to ponder but instead he peeled one side of

his overalls down enough to see where on his hip
the bee had struck. Sure enough there was a knot
there and later a bruise. There's no point to any of
this other than what happened. What happened in
the field to our neighbor then is little more than a
memory now. There is of course a poetry in it and
all of it speaking of now is happening now. Strange

to think that then is now and this applies even to
this. This being this sentence. Our neighbor had a
name. He had a real life even if it's impossible to
frame. Anything that had a life unsurprisingly has
a life still. It just takes someone alive now to be
thinking about it or not to be if they have it enough
in their bones. What could be stranger than being

alive now : with breath in your blood and with life
whatever it may be in your step. I'm certainly glad
to have it all. I'm glad to feel the sun warming my
skin as I lay here in bed up too late up in the wee
hours typing on my phone. There is always some
bee or other that needs me to feel the sun in such
unexpected moments : as if it is dying to be wanted.

Monologue on the Structures of a Bubble

What you are doing has a mysterious feel to it.
It reminds me of that waxy paper mannerly people
find around bars of Ivory soap banded together
at the bottoms of cabinets. Someday I may be cowed
by the reach of your performative contradiction,

and if I am not you can be certain somebody else
will be. There are so many ways a spark from a fire
in a weathered chimenea never accomplishes what it
sets out to do. Look up at the sky and you will be
unraveled by the ocular dynamics of its continents.

Trees sway. The retracting sunlight drenches the yard
and side of our house. For every motion there is
an imaginary countermotion among the drowsing
branches dotted with yellow, brown, orange, red
and burgundy leaves. There is fire in the evergreens.

There is water in everybody dreaming of fire. We
refine what ends we are destined to achieve. We
fill our coffee mugs with earthly oceans and we
traverse them. Whisked away to tropical paradises
our voices of real malevolence, by speaking, fade.

Into rooms other histories move while contemplating
the variegated tensions comprising a given
spherical surface. We see their ecologies swirling
and the manner of our seeing is encompassing. Into
rooms filled with the brittle enamel of patterns we

softly go. Once on the way home from work you
stopped the car and I got out to help a turtle
the rest of the way across the road. I was wearing
new shoes. Clutching the turtle firmly, I descended
the bank to the creek and imagined resolving

the momentum I had gained by landing carefully on
a flat portion of the bank. Only that portion was
a miracle of soft mud. So, I sank. So, I fell forward
letting the turtle go as I reached out with both hands
to catch myself. The turtle went flying sideways

and landed like a discus: one third in the mud
and two thirds in the air of our shared habitat. I fell
feet to knees to palms while cursing the muddy
bank for soiling my pants and for swallowing my
shoes. I drew myself up, returning to my human

posture. This was not an event, as nobody was there
to witness what occurred. Even now my telling this
is to no purpose. It is a filling of space. It is a returning.
It is a bubble rising through the boundaries of soft mud.
It is an existence framed by the eye of a monumental

seeing. Suddenly memory opens like a scroll of papyrus,
unrolling and revealing beautiful prospects, so that
I hold my hand up again, letting the light of our star
bathe it. Tomorrow I will speak on behalf of myself.
Tomorrow I will float. The idea of a turtle will be alive.

Monstrosity

My body is powered by internal combustion.
It is a fruity cluster of lust near the office cactus,
especially in that unspectacular moment
it becomes clear, like a snail learning to ignore
instances of sudden pointless touch, how much
not giving a shit takes the wind out of
cruel sails.

Scene:

this is our moment.
It is a moment
of giantism so casual nobody has noticed. Somebody must be eager
to put a bullet into our moment.
This is a perfect moment
to be alone watching a gnat crawling in circles this moment.
This moment ,
is nearly as wonderful as the Bavarian gentians of another's moment.
This is not a blue moment.
It is, on the contrary, a bottomless moment.
At some point murder is going to become the phenomena swallowing
the dislocated whales singing through this moment.
I feel disembodied when I blink. I feel exactly the way I do when pulling
a shirt over my head and waiting for the spectacular moment
when my head pops through the neck hole, or when I close my eyes
while washing my face or rinsing shampoo suds from what
counts as my hair. It feels like something terrible is going to
happen, until (and note: sleep, when it falls on me from within,

is entirely alright), until I can confirm with my eyes again, with a look approximating the sound of air being squeezed from a puffy pocket on the back of a pet toad.

File this:

under everybody has entered the atmosphere of aftermath
under the infected toy rendered the villain speechless
under smoke threading the light of goodness unbinding us
under an ordinary grub infused with mystery
under scales of mercy, scales of mercy, scales of
under mercy, mercy, mercy, mercy, mercy
under the reflected limbs of

My Double

The shape of my hand is the territory of my ear.
The direction of my foot is the song of my brain.
I am composed of organs and their natural orders.
I rest above a composite of self not knowing who
I am. Does anybody know? There are invitations
and exits at every turn even at sundown when light
from nowhere bathes objects positioned properly.

I pause thinking about the difference between
eternity and now. I like now as anybody might. There
is a caesura around the corner and I can feel it.
There is an anthem for embracing inside any cloud.
My pocket is an entire mapmaker and I am grateful.
In five minutes I will begin my physical therapy
session and my double will continue composing.

Not Mine

It saddens us to think how much the eternity of
this moment will not last how every solitary heron
will take to the air as soon as we accidentally
glance in its direction. This happens so often and
nearly every time we are on this bridge I say. Yes
it is a gesture of imagination or something nearly
so you reply. At this point a corpse sits upright in our

collective mind's coffin. How is this possible I
wonder to myself before grumbling aloud about
how odd it is that a thing buried should become
unburied. Next thing this corpse will be standing
reformed here on this bridge with us which is as
unnecessary as it is spectacular and as I finish the
thought I feel the animate presence at our elbows.

[now]

a word   is appearing
on your right hand   and again
on your left hand   [now] the same word
is shining on your forehead

in the beginning of the idea   before
you were what you   [now] are
a figure   almost a being of sorts
differentiated as you
                    before you settled

to watery simulacrum   breathing in
and out   you moved your fingers and toes
on the banks of a burbling river
                              then when
we met I became you and you became

who I was
          [now]
                    we are here

[now] we are back from the dead
[now] we are disturbing and overwhelming
whatever it is we are doing   [now]
we don't remember   forgive us

as antlers emerge   out of air
and when nobody is looking   we
are brittle as the earth under
the double vastness of northern sky

On the Trail

Not everyone who peaks
in the time of

tardigrades is worth listening to.
Some people have hands

that are naturally
slippery and that are often accompanied by

the strangest ukulele music either
of us has ever heard. I

keep waiting for the day
to get warmer even when I expect

it won't. Out of nowhere a notion
looms large and then recedes. The mystery of

love arcs fiercely between a bunched
baby rattlesnake and the beak of a mockingbird.

The Opposite of Vikings

Inside the mouth we waited and we stretched out
and we laid down and we fell asleep and we dreamed
the mouth around us was kindly disappearing. Upon
waking we were thankful despite being still inside
the mouth. If you need us to be here we will try
to live our lives whatever may be left of them and
however little they may be worth in the scheme of

existence to keep you from distress and from
any further hunting. We know what it is like to be
hungry and we offer ourselves to you whoever you
may be to keep you fed and to keep you well.
This sounded so much like nonsense our would-be
devourer wept and pitifully spit us out. We are
sorry to have made you cry we chorused forever.

Our Wilderness

Something about a lack of wildness had us
examining the landscape more intently. Clouds
were getting shiftier by the minute, and

the old horse up the hill neighed into the wind.
It was certainly reasonable to ask, as ribbons
of water slipped over the stone wall at the visible

end of a small lake, who were we? The world
was an animal showing up, as if from nowhere,
and lying like a puddle in the clover of our

yard. There was hair on a shoulder. There was
heat in the air. There was recoil and the kind
of advice that can make a difference. Later,

the cardinal will reanimate the top wire of
our deer fence. Just like a friend reconfiguring
the forest floor rises with antlers full of life.

Out of Earth

The figure appeared out of the ribcage   of a tree
where we were crouched in the ferns.   They were
vacillating between dark and light   and between
muscular and slender. We love   crouching in ferns
and feeling a desire to merge in the leaf mold with
earth underneath | while beholding such a figure.

We love the feeling of richness. It feels like biting

into a pear picked from our own orchard. We love

holding our hands in front of our faces in sunlight.
The figure that appeared out of the ribcage of a
tree seems to be connected to the sunlight but in
ways more substantial than every other thing or
person. The figure was so full of light that the ferns
doubled in size | as we each became real doubles.

Phoenixlike

People living inside and outside of fences
are eating or choking down entire meals,
reading whole feeds or tomes the size
of the complete works of plato,
while i am complaining about them all

for being so gratuitous. Honestly, what kind
of person completes anything. I just want
to bite an apple while sipping from a cup of coffee
that has turned room temperature. I will
never think of anything grand or accomplish

a thing of note. I am less a platonist and more
an informalist who is almost as able as
a variation on a meme to be consistently
so. One minute i am on my feed too
only to wonder what is going to happen

when the road between this unincorporated
community and the neighboring proper
town of springfield, tn has been repaved. They
are working on it. I know because we just got hung
in the sap of friday afternoon traffic. This is

a field after all were somebody is waiting to
feel what happens. Not knowing if i can,
i take off my shoes to make an image (being
the inconsistently inconsistent person i
sometimes am) i imagine will never be unmade,

here where a fence runs between the earth
of our neighbor's yard and ours. Like goodness.
Like the marrow in the ash of bones. Like
tenderness as unexpected as it is deserved. We
will be gone before we can dare arrive.

Poem of Thankfulness

Today i am thankful for morning frost
touched by sunlight and sparkling

on lawns and fields   I am thankful too
for you and the warmth provided to my feet

inside ordinary socks and shoes and the way
the music of your voice enters my ears

and warms my heart leaving this planet of ours
spinning (if only slightly) more easily;

and i will consider how the world is good
difficult and good and how a lifetime

is both too short and too long
and how the injured heart cannot heal but

as researchers in sweden have discovered
the muscle of our disadvantaged organ also can

and does slowly replenish itself   Today
when the bigness of the sky asks whoever

is standing beneath it are you ready
the gray trees drowsing and temporarily losing

the last of their burnt sienna leaves will say yes
and you will say yes and i will say yes too

Poem without a Title

A figure sits quietly on the shadowed earth
underneath the spreading branches of
the tree of the mind. Through long night
an owl calls with spaced out, singular
cries. It wants to know who is still alive,

although this is impossible to tell, as each
fragile and wounded side is volleying
fury at the other. If we are not careful, who
we are will vanish into who we are
becoming and a shadow lacking all sense

of accountability will rise and swallow
both figure and tree. There are reasons
beyond the reasons we know, reasons swift
as a door left ajar all night. Where mosses
and lichens and vines grow, the river is

softly burbling. It's true nobody knows
whether an owl that has called into
the night will call again. Somebody assumes
features as if they can do nothing else.
Blink twice and you will arrive like a wind.

Put These in Your Pocket

I am taller when I am with you : you my star
both close and distant. I love the closeness of
your closeness. I love the wave we make while
casually going along together. A pine tree is a
lovely thing when the door is locked and the
windows too. Every beautiful thing enters by
skylight. Decorative grass enters this way. We

have our own culture and we share it freely. It
is as if we cannot help ourselves. In fact we
cannot help ourselves. If there is no sustaining
this around there is still the most sustaining
this. Us. There is still a wing of goodness over
everything transmuting loss into abundance and
the weight of old stones into the life of lichen.

The Question

Everything here comes out of here. For example
while leaning into a listicle I feel more confident
in revealing my favorite flavor of ice cream after
the sky falls. What is the sky. In ancient Chinese
philosophy the sky was one meaning of *tzu-jan* or
heaven. Then as now people looked into the sky

and saw immensity. Chuang Tzu even wrote about

an enormous bird called P'eng. Not that anybody

cares about P'eng these days. Still : a real myth
never dies. We all know this even when we have
temporarily forgotten. If you don't believe me
ask P'eng or yourself. Like I said everything here
comes out of here and that includes you in all
ways and whether you ask the question or not.

Remoteness

People looking for the sun rarely find it. Instead
they see stars and catch glimpses of those celestial
bodies that merely reflect light. No derogation is
meant. The distinction between bodies capable
of generating light and those that only reflect is
entirely factual. How else could spotting the sun
be difficult. Light for all its power is exceedingly

tender and who can fault it for acting according
to its nature for being there despite invisibility.
Life is nothing if not filled to overflowing with
craft as if the future is constantly losing its own
edge like dawn. The sun can obscure whatever
it brings to living light by being obscured. Know
yourself and you will find the sun everywhere.

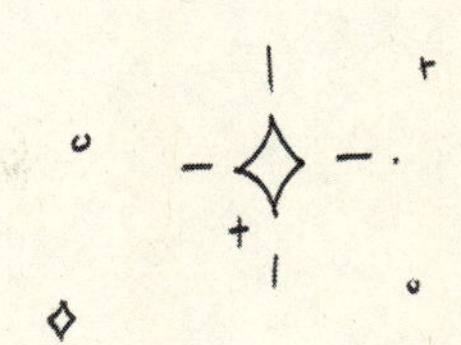

The River

By cliffs, in the room of morning, soft data
moved like a weeping wildfire. Nobody believed
it, so it died and then quickly reanimated as
an emblem abandoned near a modest, well-kept
villa. Similarly, you have already drifted into the first
stage and now might as well fill your rain boots.

I am looking over the railing with you at mint.
It grows profusely, almost unnaturally, as we swim
through its scent, which has been unlocked by
a waxing sun. All of this reminds me of the time
an absolute stranger pressed a vision into the minds
of everybody in our vicinity. We laughed dustily

as it happened. Probably this is half predictable
considering how we kept encountering, as we ventured
deeper and deeper into the proverbial woods, new,
but empty, snail shells. Those shells only left us asking
ourselves and each other, Where are the snails?
If you look the other way, you will see me looking

at you from a simultaneous dimension. You will
feel the pulse of my efforts as a comforting thing,
and, feeling it, will recognize it as your own. Still,
nothing is closer to what matters than what is inherent
in what already exists. What already exists rises along
a vector of curious tenderness. If, atop a tall pylon,

the mother of a brood of goslings begins feeling
restless about passing humans, it might be time to
leave their nest and enter the larger safety of the river.
There, hawks may descend, talons slicing through
eponymous air, and wild dogs may howl their hungers
into the starry panorama of a semi-navigable night.

Rolling with the Schadenfreude

Thank you for throwing your big goofy cat in my lap
and regardless how small the scale for being
the Disaster Gargoyle you are. Without you stars
would vanish from space at random and one of them
would eventually be our sun. Thank you for scrunching
up your shoulders over the duress of others and for
admitting you want to see them hurt. The hurt
of others will make your world more bearable especially
if those others are vulnerable to any onslaught you stir.
In forests of post-apocalyptic tribulations where frogs
croak out songs suddenly from branches rain silences
the glory of wings. Tonight you will fail to fall
into the hell you deserve to fall into due to the size
of Sandhill Cranes. These cranes will pluck out your eyes.

Sailing

Today you will reorder yesterday for the sake of
tomorrow. Something will bubble and froth behind
your left ear leaving behind a sensation like when
you first bite into a perfect and juicy apple. I have
an eye and a tongue and a soul for juice and so feel
bold about this assertion. Even when we are apart
my mind fills up with juice while thinking about you.

You are better than my favorite sweater : the one covered
in images of the moon : the one that threads through
real space. I like space too and must decree that
between it and you you are the realer. I was floating
across space while pondering the heft of this and feeling
the greater you of you and all the ways my deeper self
likes wearing the bigness of such data on its sleeves.

The Scholars

That's so cringey the scholar said. Absolutely
another said. Before anyone can even say what
if anything is happening it is probably worth
constructing a foundational point of departure
if that is you care about the theory of absence.

The scholars looked behind each other and
were unable to determine who or perhaps what
had made that last remark. They felt so old
older than mountains which of course are not
particularly old in the scheme of things. Who

cares whether or not it is raining in distant
places. We have all the water we need at hand.
Anybody is brimming with fortune before they
are capable of creation. If the reason life is
good is simultaneously the same and different

why not return to the long city. It was time for
breakfast and more scholars had joined the
initial pair. We know how to live dangerously
the pair announced to the others. That's so
great and we believe you the newcomers said.

Sea Sparkle

You can try your best and still not see it.

The Season of Innocence

I was getting my ass kicked
in the passenger seat

while a handful of leaves
deepened in hue while

falling further into
autumn. It's almost as if our

pumpkin vine was waiting for
weather like this you said as

you pulled the windshield shade
away from my face and folded it into

a circle before reaching back and
stuffing it into the pocket

behind my seat. Ooooh I love circles
as much as anyone I replied.

Second Time Is a Charm

The way the grass is growing today is rude.
This is probably no surprise considering
the length of our albatross longings, as
we run into the new plastic of complexity
and enjoy the strangeness of a net effect.

Anyway, how a starfish decides which way
to move is a headless, if not a mindless,
venture, one that gives a smoother surface
to symbiotic relationships between the organs
of organisms and their rudderless drivers.

Those mornings when the sky is orange,
a glow drifts through air being stippled
by birdsong. It is easy to hope unpleasantness
will disappear. Probably none of us likes it
and there is a smell to how it makes us feel

that is almost as cloying as the rough fabric
a pair of pants may be cut from. Later, if night
reembraces day, we will have more than we
imagined possible to discuss. Night is richer
than morning. It is a miracle converging.

Soft Spot

The middle ground is so hot you said. I disagree
at least some of the time I said. I was thinking
about being in a candy store and reaching both
hands into a bin of candy which I never did even
as a child. Instead I only thought about doing it.

Is this bus going next door somebody asked the
person napping beside them. The napper woke
and yawned. I apologize the napper said I didn't
hear your question. The person repeated while
stepping forward to board the bus as if where it

was going didn't matter and the napper nodded
yes. That is hot too the middle ground said. Are
we playing you're hot I'm hot you said. No said
the middle ground I'm just letting you know how
I've always felt. That's very kind of you you said.

Sonnet

If I say I am an American it will suddenly be clear
I do not know what grain I am working

against. What begins underneath the other
side is folly almost is news almost as

what we already know or should know dances
in headlines before us. Anybody looking for an anecdote

can dote on the old barns dotting the landscape so
profusely. Anybody looking for a properly licensed technician will

want to dip a toe into crystal creeks.
We are busy turning

the words we nearly hear nearly as hairy
as sumac and who doesn't want that.

Who doesn't want the comingled juices of our anthems blowing
through their valves like wild lights that are shining from selectively
crepuscular stars.

Sonnet

The color of your shirt extends to the landscape
first. Then it extends to the illusion frequently
called the sky. Now that the consequences are
looming hard you feel as fulfilled as anybody

would. You are learning to dream like you used
to and you know it. That is why your shirt
is ballooning. And you you are drifting as if life
is what happens only while music is playing.

In the next scene I am with you and we are
rolling through the rolling hills. It is that time
of the season when trees are mostly bare yet
some are still holding leaves so gorgeous in

the light any heart might joyfully leap. Driving
together is such a miracle and we each know it.

A Stranger in Ica

I am looking at, rather than through,
the maps I have drawn out from inside myself,
examining them as objects I can now
appreciate. It is like that time a stranger

went to Ica and strolled between
the ocean and the cliffs. The way things
are there is not the way they are here,
the stranger thought while strolling.   I am

unsure how I know this, and now you, by
extension and like a rabbit being drawn from
a hat, are, too.   Returning to the stranger
and reflecting briefly on the thought, we find

divaricating types of imagination open to us.

They feel like cards falling from our sleeves.

Succulents

Upon further questioning we decided to wait until
the entire entity unfolded. Every molecule
of it I mean. Some of us maintained good functionality.
Still, the older fliers among us
were prone to wandering off while

the rest of us were sleeping.
Nights in strange lands are punctuated by quantities
of dreamers and rain is gathering
force above a teacup. Those of us who are
halfway are falling asleep standing or

sitting but are awake whenever we are
lying down. Through caverns of
night we bow in reverence to strengths inside
ourselves, strengths exceeding the reach
of our abilities. Like a new bond emerging from edges

of icy archipelagos, driving
mechanical orders of imagination, like the bitter dust
of souls, like a heart covered by a fist
of sand, we are mingling the crown with
the carnivorous roots of flowers, as danger widens

its lenses. Our destiny is no longer manifest
as we once believed. We are
releasing another kind of life, a life measured against
the size of what we do not know
and cannot imagine from our cocoon

of ferns and fire. When we reenter
using recalculations, smoke
surrounds us along the wired shores
of forgiveness. Our gentleness
is a current that no single vessel delivers.

The Susquehanna by Moonlight

All the lovers a single chain has joined together
—Guillaume Apollinaire

Tiny feathers
are drifting through air
shared by opposing reinforcements
cluttering heads. Before lowering your
platform helmet,

consider what your breath
and blood are doing out beyond the edge of
these woods. Consider how coyotes are calling
each to each
at acceptable distances

from where you are.
When it is night, you will be sleeping
with your bedroom window open. In your dreams coyotes
will walk calmly past
your unlit window. In your dreams

you will feel their fur softly
inside the ventricles
of your soul. Their fur
will be a willow stick
shoved in earth merely to mark

a spot, until, to the surprise of all, that stick, sprig by
leaf by sprig by leaf, becomes
a mature willow. The leaves of your dreams will
droop and mingle
with the leaves

of ordinary grass.
These leaves will be
the living
eyes and ears
when you wake.

Thank You

Like an animal displaced by logging
roaming your yard. Like

a sudden swarm at your elbow when
night with its next breath expires.

Like messages from a distant friend
populating your dreams once you pass through

the secret door. Here you are making
your moment having grown tired of

waiting. You open a book at random and
find life. You close it and put it away

as the lava cools and the ash settles.
Entering this candle flame has many

rewards. A bird in your hand spreads its wings
and flies with its might into pages of forever.

The Thanksgiving Cactus

Here in a chair
in a cozy corner of this room,
under the glow of a lamp,
with the sun replaced by
the moon   hanging
boldly in the sky, I pause
to consider the small pink buds
of a toothed cactus,

and I pause to consider
the moon as well,   although
it is too far away to touch,
and in my pausing I feel
as if I am a wave on the ocean
or a seed   pulsing
in a warmer season, now
that the leaves have gone

from most of the trees, now
that frost dusts the brittle grass
most mornings, now
that weather keeps us more
indoors,   so that we are more
able to be together, more
together, even during moments
in lamplight   like this one.

The Three Trees at Hudimesnil

I shouldn't be doing this the room said. I didn't
know rooms could do anything much less
talk about it I said. Well that's on you the room
said but at least you know better now. A person
wearing a pink shirt gray jacket and beige pants
was stroking their chin. Another one was wearing
a mask. A big part of living is matching what

you do or say to what else is being done or said
by others. The difficulty is in knowing where to
draw the line. For example the philosophical and
conceptual mind desires to be included with its
casual counterparts such as the need for rest and
idleness. We are living through imperfect times
and clearly deserve all the shit we'll give ourselves.

To Dust

For Christopher Phelps

No one knows why their small bag contains a handful of stones
that appear to be from another world. Even as it feels as if
something is an answer, our cherished dragon scales still crumble
to dust. I want to write a letter to dust, only I have no idea

what to say. Often, I imagine learning the subtle contours of
the next thing will help, although I understand the definition
of futility. Short of writing a letter I cannot write, there is nothing
I can do, even as a current is flowing around and through me.

Somebody from somewhere once said that life is what happens
between elliptical poles that arrive in the form of baths. It is
not quite as absurd as it seems, although it is absurd. When the
sun goes down and the stars begin swimming, I like thinking

of infinite ways the impossible can happen. I like reading pages
as candles burn down, or as a lamp or two glows peacefully on.
I like opening one eye and then another and discovering shared
worlds are still intact, even as so many beyond our hedges and

underneath our flowerpots pursue singular futures. Deception so
often lies at the joint while threading into each wayward seam,
as if no price is too great in the face of the promise our new fields
deliver. Even if a cloud hangs over Grandfather Mountain, as

buntings flash their variegated and occasionally inimical indigos
over long and wavering grasses, as they will someday, I will desire
to always live as I do now. I hold my hand up to the testimony
of this and every star. There is a power before us all that is also

appearing with and after us. Still, we wait, desiring to offer each
bounty eluding us. Why are we so devoured by powers greater
than ourselves? Why do we reach to touch, in place of believing,
this dust filling our bones, unlike the next of our alien species?

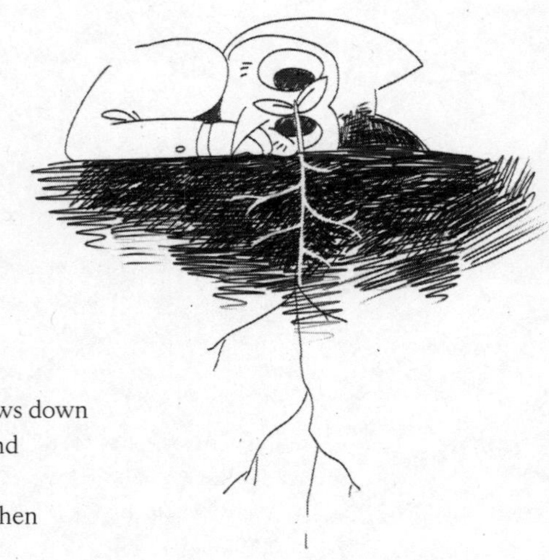

To Earth

Complexity of view flows down
one side of the valley and

up the other. If this is when
I am, this is what I will

write while considering the construct
of the forest floor. Trees tell

clearer tales when sap has
returned to root. The greater the

distance from them, the closer
their fallen leaves are. Meanwhile,

the closer a walnut is to point of
vantage, the easier it is to imagine

it having a future life, if
it settles hard enough to earth.

To January

I open my heart to what is here.

A sky. Two kinds of air
and sunlight. An entire world.

All the endless things I love
and the things I disagree with
that somehow remain of interest.

I open my heart like you
open your own. Still,
I would rather not put thought
into how I remember hidden lakes.

We were sleeping when the fog
swallowed the woods behind our house.
Now that we are awake, it is as if

nothing at all happened.

Today

We are here to collect the most
beautiful starlight around.

From the sides of mountains, we
exit the doors set to keep us

hale and hearty. The fire of our
hair is gray, and we are smoldering like

on the hearth. Remembering
is in hand each time we open

one of ours. Night draws itself
firmly around us. It is filling

with songs of snow. The world
as we know and feel it is

ancient and goofy. Where we
readily are becomes a furthering of far.

Tomorrow

Under this leaf I am my own
allegory. There is a story

running backward across my
life, and I can feel it. There is a

place inside the clustered
boulders covered in the lichens

they are covered in. The boulders,
I mean, and not the place.

A place, as you know, can never
be covered in anything. There are

clouds drifting various directions.
Welcome to the magic that must not

and can not and will not fail.
It will fit inside and carry you.

Untitled

So much of what is needed, is
needed without our knowing. Words are
reordering, lines are reshaping themselves, almost,
while articulating some shifting thing or other. What
any of it means is

as tangential as grass near
a bank, rising to sway
above the water of a river. Meanwhile,
and clearly, the seam, the joint is
the kind of space anyone might feel. Space

connects as much as it divides. Space
is a bouquet of real balloons drifting inside a
low cloud. One night, while
sitting on our back deck and looking up into
the wheeling of the sky, we

heard behind you something, something
larger lunging in hard pursuit of
something smaller, and we
each tuned our ears while turning as
the smaller thing got away into

the privet at the edge of the woods. You
had caught sight of the larger thing, and so, as I leaned
farther back while returning my gaze to
the sky, you began describing
and pondering the unexpected shape of

the larger thing, silhouetted darker
against the immensity of the night's darkness. It looked
like a coyote, you said then. Perhaps it was
a black coyote, I think now, as smoke drifts from
a neighbor's fire, in a thicket of gentle rain.

Visitation

I look at our salt lamp, and my mind
wanders associatively. It is clear
some prefer reading to read to reading
perhaps as much as I do. There are always gulls
gliding over given oceans, always

new frontiers to existing rhizomes,
always inhalations and exhalations. But what
do I know? I sit scrying a book for
anything to write about next, while pondering,
indirectly, how so many write poems

about writing poems. Whether I
ponder or wander
between or through associations, as I scry
the entire book of a world surrounding me, but only
unto myself some say, depends on what? Something only

they can determine? If the required
amount of energy is not endogenously present
all the way to an end, who will open
a hand in mercy? That night we were
wakened by the terrible sounds, rising from

a small field beyond a stretch of brambles, of a wild pig
devouring a quail's nest. The mother cried and cried, without
achieving her desired result. Later,
the same pig, or another, came
to snort around and then to press

and run a bristly side along
one side of our tent, so that both sides
bowed inward and inward, as
the horrible, snorting beast grunted softly in
the crystal glow of moonlight.

Voice from a Dream

I never knew what an aurora was until I saw one
spreading above me like a tremendous albeit
amorphous blanket. The way it gripped the thing
inside the heart is impossible to say in words.
Yet here I am doing a version of exactly that.
When you consider it the word tremendous is

itself clearly tremendous as all words are of

course and in their multifarious ways. Sparks

from a cloth of flame tend to set off various
difficult-to-describe fates. Thus the aurora I
did not see despite what I have said. Imagine
strolling the quadrangle at some university or
other you have probably visited. It will give
you a hint of how I felt then as much as now.

Waiting by the Door

Under a blanket as transparent as itself
and as piled up as junk in a yard

you found your future. The numbers on the clock moved
in their usual procession. A quake rose

through the earth like a wave
with patches on its elbows before disappearing into

the weave of an unspectacular
upholstery fabric. The signal had grown long

as memory even as it fades
like notes of music perfect for

the moment. Later in the night
trees swayed and knew they belonged

knew they were integral to the alchemy a reader
desires at least some of the time. And here it is.

In the future when the box is opened
mummies will invade the neighborhood. Comets will fall

on top of that from the aching vastness of space.
They will be filled with glades and fjords

and trails and shrubberies as familiar to us
as we are to the grimacing windows of ourselves.

The Way It Started

Somebody whispered once into my ear. It was
one of those afternoons and I felt like making
mischief of expectations. Have I succeeded
I wondered aloud to the absence left by the
whisperer. You know people do not appreciate
mischief a nearby tree seemed to say as wind
shifted its dainty branches. But how does wind

do anything I thought as I paused allowing
the whisper further into my bones. At the apex
of this I fell asleep and imagined dreaming of
waking reconfigured so that each aspect of myself
differed even as I remained entirely the same
person. This is very strange I thought after really
waking as my voice came from my own mouth.

The Weather in a Place

I cannot remember the last time it was this cold
for this long. For example there are as my alarm
sounds its final time inches of ice on top of
the rainwater accumulated in the large grey
storage bin on our back porch. On top of that
there is snow. I am not writing this for any reason
I know of yet. Water and ice are not particularly
significant. Neither is writing. But I like to let
words fall into view like pellets of ice or drifting
flakes of snow while thinking back on days of
insignificant rain. What is it I am hoping to
connect that has not already been connected by
someone else in the fact of a long dream? Does
one more set of fourteen lines make a difference?

There is also this morning the issue of dry grass.
Its blades and stalks are peeking occasionally
through the inches of ice and snow. Winter can
be heartless in this way. It can leave us without
the traces and markers and signs we depend on.
In a dream I reached out for the solid form in
front of me only to feel it fade through the frame
of my grasp. What do I have that is not dream
even now? Night is present in the opaque glow
of this morning act because like all poles it is
collapsing into the assertions it or something like
it insists on making in relation to any evidence.
I could stand on this ice and settle all my weight
into it and my soles would remain above the grass.

Between sleep and waking there is no difference
if there is a beach of dreams connecting land
to ocean or if there is fire inside the strange ice
of a triple sun. I move across water in my little
kayak like a whirligig before going under. A glass
of milk is another kind of miracle. Like tomorrow
with every fenced-out thing curled inside it it
is impossible to make pressure build. Tomorrow
is seedlike like that. Like this. Fictions of form
and amplifications of shadow contribute what
then? If you too cannot say decompose your will
and lie down and become dust with me. If you
too are entirely less than heroic and somehow
more than unheroic let your life bloom new cold.

Welcome Back

While not dreaming what am I doing. Getting
lost among the leaves it seems. But why even.

Why not let the leaves get lost among me as
I lose myself among them enjoying the real

effervescence of mutual mutability. One night
an owl called out. What is it saying I asked

myself as one does in situations like this. As
if I could or had a right to know. People we

forget remember us all the time. The bench
empty under the nearly leafless tree is probably

lonely. I could ask it but then I would be left
holding one too many things. There are days

anybody might feel like rolling up their heart
and drawing what goes with it into a shell.

Window

At what point
within the geography

do you realize
you deserve to stay

alive? A wound appears.
You are in a forest

at night and marveling
at the bioluminescence

of its myriad organic features
excepting yourself. Waking

you turn on a lamp
and find yourself waking

still more. A fern explodes
in your mind. On a new

mountain you recalibrate shore
in range of ways you might.

The Winner

We were arguing to find out what
our real feelings could be. I

placed large olives on every other
fingertip. You felt

the preciousness of the air around your
second pair of ears. It was spring

until it wasn't. I never knew
people like you could do the

things you do you said. Then a knife
opened in the heart of your

mind. The winner will have to die first
I said. Then you win you said.

Thank you I said. I
always wanted to be first at something.

With a Bubble around Your Head

from the eye   of a turtle shell
from the tongue   of a lodestone
    when a storm is   impending
from the past

                    when

the Merrillian ghost   of a tiny hand
pulls a plug on what you say   your life
has come to   insisting   you cannot
possibly   know what   you know

now your shoe has become a raft
and you are adrift on it   you who
keep echoing more than yourself
to yourself as you breathe   alien

Wrapped around Eleanor

This isn't a patch unless we don't know what
is happening or how Eleanor, in the sinew
of the moment, is. Presently, we are falling into
the sensuality of what isn't, into what is free
inside the taste of honeycomb. Unable to say
what this is like, we are gazing happily at branches
exploding into seasonal outer blooming. Warmth

from the sun is almost real, especially when it
touches the living needles of pine trees so their
scent softens the breeze of an afternoon. Fast
is the preferred posture. Fast makes pollen land
prolifically on another earth. We found Eleanor,
exactly the way she found herself, with rabbits
running through her hair like untamable charms.

Yesterday

We left the party glowing. You forgot
your favorite cap and I

my latest pair of fangs. Now that
we are in the real world, filled

with things covered in
moss and ferns, there are

so many waves it all becomes
eventual ocean. This is a long world,

especially now that its scope,
like a stray pinecone, is

happening. Something
reminded us both how cheery

we can be under circumstances
more favorable. We did not know what.

Acknowledgements

I am grateful to the editors of the Propel Disability Poetry Series for believing in this collection and to Cortney Lamar Charleston, Flower Conroy, Greg Dember, Mónica Gomery, Carolyn Hembree, K. Iver, Dora Malech, Airea D. Matthews, Naomi Shihab Nye, Kiana Shaley, Richard Siken, and Jamie Thurman. Thank you as well to the editors of these publications where the following poems were published.

Academy of American Poets, *Poem-a-Day*: "The Genie Speaks"
American Poetry Journal: "[now]"
American Poetry Review: "Another Impulse," "A Candle in the Night," "The Fruits of Our Labor," "Our Wilderness," "A Stranger in Ica," "To Dust"
Annulet: "Out of Earth"
Bennington Review: "The Winner"
Biscuit Hill: "Already Fossils," "Both Hands in the Jar"
Blazing Stadium: "Behind a Home," "Distractible Maybe," "The Weather in a Place"
Blood Orange Review: "Poem of Thankfulness"
The Boiler: "Cabinet of Wonders," "Currently Nobody"
Columbia Journal: "Monstrosity"
The Cortland Review: "Forever Tympanum"
EcoTheo Review: "To January"
The Florida Review: "Folding Leaves"
Grateful.org: "The Thanksgiving Cactus"
Gulf Coast: "Kiddo"
Harvard Divinity Bulletin: "The Susquehanna by Moonlight"
The Hopkins Review: "The Fairy Citadel"
Iterant: "Evolutionary," "The Life of the Moon," "The Way it Started"
Journal Nine: "Wrapped around Eleanor"
Mantis: A Journal of Poetry, Criticism, and Translation: "Rolling with the Schadenfreude"
Nine Mile Magazine: "All Our Spoons at Once," "Beauty and Shadow," "Birth Magic," "Eel Feels," "Have a Great Day," "Hymn for Lighting the Sky," "The Idle Remark," "Lick the Toad," "Phoenixlike," "Remoteness," "The Scholars," "Today," "The Three Trees at Hudimesnil," "With a Bubble around Your Head," "Waiting by the Door"
North American Review: "Tomorrow"
Poetry: "Be Monster," "Cuddly in Camo"
Poetry Wales: "Hello Vessel"
The Rumpus: "Envy Seas," "Gloves in Autumn," "My Double"
The Scores: "Fireflies"
The South Carolina Review: "The River," "Sonnet"

Southern Humanities Review: "A Cup of Tea," "To Earth," "Welcome Back"
The Southern Review: "Early Saturday Evening"
swamp pink: "Yesterday"
Tupelo Quarterly: "From the Root," "Holding a Pinecone"
Vagabond City: "Sailing"
Western Humanities Review: "The Cabin Mirror"
Wordgathering: A Journal of Disability Poetry and Literature: "A History of Leaves," "Monologue on the Structures of a Bubble," "Second Time is a Charm," "Succulents"
Zócalo Public Square: "Poem without a Title"
Zoeglossia, *Poem of the Week:* "Ask Me Later"

How to Love the World: Poems of Gratitude and Hope, edited by James Crews, Storey Press, 2021: "A Candle in the Night"
Poetry Daily, May 28, 2021: "A Cup of Tea"
On timemedecine.org, 2022: "A Candle in the Night"
The American Sonnet: An Anthology of Poems and Essays, edited by Dora Malech and Laura T. Smith, University of Iowa Press, 2023: "Kiddo"
The Wonder of Small Things: Poems of Peace and Renewal, edited by James Crews, Storey Press, 2023: "Poem of Thankfulness"

Photo by Daniel Meigs

Nathan Spoon is an autistic poet with learning disabilities and written expression disorder whose poems and essays have appeared in the Academy of American Poets' *Poem-a-Day*, *American Poetry Review*, *Bennington Review*, *Gulf Coast*, *Poetry*, *Poetry Daily*, *The Southern Review*, and *swamp pink*. He is editor of *Queerly* and an ally of timemedicine.org.